Inspiration

WOMEN'S
VOICES

Poetry & Letters

Publisher and Creative Director: Nick Wells
Commissioning Editor: Polly Prior
Senior Project Editor: Josie Mitchell
Art Director and Layout Design: Mike Spender
Digital Design and Production: Chris Herbert

FLAME TREE PUBLISHING

6 Melbray Mews
London SW6 3NS
United Kingdom

www.flametreepublishing.com
First published 2019

19 21 23 22 20
1 3 5 7 9 10 8 6 4 2

Every effort has been made to contact copyright holders. In the event of
an oversight the publishers would be glad to rectify any omissions in future
editions of this book.

A CIP record for this book is available from the British Library upon request.

ISBN 978-1-78755-277-7

Printed in China | Created, Developed & Produced in the United Kingdom

Inspiration

WOMEN'S
VOICES

Poetry & Letters

Introduction by
Rebecca Tamás

FLAME TREE
PUBLISHING

CONTENTS

INTRODUCTION

In her essay *A Room of One's Own*, published in 1929, Virginia Woolf describes a hidden realm of muted female poets – women whose frustrated desire for creativity makes them appear in history as witches, wise women, the mothers of great men. These women, whose writerly powers were suppressed and subdued by the societies around them expressed themselves in other, secret forms: in magic, care and mischief.

But it seems that the women Woolf described – the women straining at the restraints of their society, did not always remain entirely mute. Because what this book demonstrates is that there is a hidden realm of female poets who *did* manage to put pen to paper; ignored, supressed, but existent. Women who got the chance to write, even against the impossible odds of their birth, gender, and situation. Because of these pioneering women, we can encounter the strangeness, multiplicity, diversity, variety and power, of female experience put into words throughout the ages.

This innovative collection brings that neglected history of female poetry and letters – from the ancient worlds of Sappho and Tao-yün, to the urban modernity of Lola Ridge – into the light. The poems of the collection come from the traditions of multiple languages and nations, giving us female voices from the Americas, Europe, Africa and Asia; demonstrating not only that women have been crafting and shaping language since the earliest written cultures, but that they have been doing so across every continent. In this book, the phenomenally varied history of female knowledge and song can pour into the English language.

The collection follows four loose themes, which give fascinating insights into the endless variety of women's experience and selfhood. In the chapter Spirituality, Art and Nature, women explore the succour of their experience of god, and contemplate the peace, and sometimes exhilaration, nature brings –

> Among the rocks – an empty hollow,
> Secret, still, mysterious!
>
> Times and Seasons, what things are you
> Bringing to my life ceaseless change?
>
> Tao-yün (A.D. 400)

In the chapter A Place and Time in the World, we find poems of travel, place and voyaging. These poems search out fresh horizons, and inscribe women's experience of space, belonging and alienation –

> Night-walkers pass along the sidewalks.
> The city is squalid and sinister,
> With the silver-barred street in the midst,
> Slow-moving,
> A river leading nowhere.

Amy Lowell (1874–1925)

Following from this, the chapter Love and Desire allows women to give *their* perspective on the endless entanglements of love, sexuality, passion and friendship. In these poems, women do not remain silent and demure, but allow their emotions and desires powerful expression in verse –

> Let fire weigh heavy and the earth weigh light;
>
> Sooner than might another know my love.
> Born was I but to grant you all thereof:
> For you alone I live, and for you, die.

Madeleine de l'Aubespine (1546–96)

In the final section, Femininity and Womanhood, we find poems, letters, and even songs, which explore the everyday texture of female experience. In these poems, women turn their gaze on themselves; considering who they are and might become, and using language itself to find spiritual and intellectual freedom.

Such a freedom we see in the poem, 'Emancipation', by American poet Emily Dickinson. This poem makes clear that whatever limits have been put on women by society: limits on their bodies, their time, their energy, their ability to speak; women's minds, our minds, have always flown free. This book is a testament to that inner flight –

> No rack can torture me,
> My soul's at liberty
> Behind this mortal bone
> There knits a bolder one

Rebecca Tamás

SPIRITUALITY, ART AND NATURE

CHRISTIAN SONNET

Let my war turn to peace eternal, Lord,
And my heart, hard as ice, melt in your fire;
Let me be moved, henceforth, by one desire;
To heed your call, tread your just path, restored.

Vanquish the passions of my soul's discord;
Purge my mind of transgression, dark and dire;
Accord my eyes your light, unveiled; inspire
In me your graces, secret of heaven's reward.

In you alone my every hope I place:
Great though my wrongs, yet greater still that grace
That fails not who cries unto you her dole.

Redeem my spirit; keep it evermore:
Give it the wings of faith, that it may soar
Aloft, cleansed of life's sins that tempt my soul.

Madeleine de l'Aubespine (1546–96)

Ave Maria

Hail Mary,
O authoress of life,
rebuilding up salvation's health,
for death you have disturbed,
that serpent crushed
to whom Eve raised herself,
her neck outstretched
with puffed-up pride.
That serpent's head you ground to dust
when heaven's Son of God you bore,
on whom has breathed
God's Spirit.

O sweet and most beloved
mother, hail!
Your Son
from heaven sent you gave unto the world:
on whom has breathed
God's Spirit.

Glory be to the Father and to the Son
and to the Holy Spirit.

On him has breathed
God's Spirit.

Hildegard of Bingen (1098–1179)

STARS

Ah! why, because the dazzling sun
Restored my earth to joy
Have you departed, every one,
And left a desert sky?

All through the night, your glorious eyes
Were gazing down in mine,
And with a full heart's thankful sighs
I blessed that watch divine!

I was at peace, and drank your beams
As they were life to me
And revelled in my changeful dreams
Like petrel on the sea.

Thought followed thought – star followed star
Through boundless regions on,
While one sweet influence, near and far,
Thrilled through and proved us one.

Why did the morning rise to break
So great, so pure a spell,
And scorch with fire the tranquil cheek
Where your cool radiance fell?

Blood-red he rose, and arrow-straight,
His fierce beams struck my brow;
The soul of Nature sprang elate,
But mine sank sad and low!

My lids closed down – yet through their veil
I saw him blazing still;
And bathe in gold the misty dale,
And flash upon the hill.

I turned me to the pillow then
To call back Night, and see
Your worlds of solemn light, again
Throb with my heart and me!

It would not do – the pillow glowed
And glowed both roof and floor,
And birds sang loudly in the wood,
And fresh winds shook the door.

The curtains waved, the wakened flies
Were murmuring round my room,
Imprisoned there, till I should rise
And give them leave to roam.

O Stars and Dreams and Gentle Night;
O Night and Stars return!
And hide me from the hostile light
That does not warm, but burn –

That drains the blood of suffering men;
Drinks tears, instead of dew:
Let me sleep through his blinding reign,
And only wake with you!

Emily Brontë (1818–48)

To Flush, My Dog (Extract)

Loving friend, the gift of one,
Who, her own true faith, hath run,
Through thy lower nature ;
Be my benediction said
With my hand upon thy head,
Gentle fellow-creature!

Like a lady's ringlets brown,
Flow thy silken ears adown
Either side demurely,
Of thy silver-suited breast
Shining out from all the rest
Of thy body purely.

Darkly brown thy body is,
Till the sunshine, striking this,
Alchemize its dulness, –
When the sleek curls manifold
Flash all over into gold,
With a burnished fulness.

Underneath my stroking hand,
Startled eyes of hazel bland
Kindling, growing larger, –
Up thou leapest with a spring,
Full of prank and curvetting,
Leaping like a charger.

Leap! thy broad tail waves a light ;
Leap! thy slender feet are bright,
Canopied in fringes.
Leap – those tasselled ears of thine
Flicker strangely, fair and fine,
Down their golden inches

Yet, my pretty sportive friend,
Little is 't to such an end
That I praise thy rareness !
Other dogs may be thy peers
Haply in these drooping ears,
And this glossy fairness.

But of thee it shall be said,
This dog watched beside a bed

Day and night unweary, –
Watched within a curtained room,
Where no sunbeam brake the gloom
Round the sick and dreary.

Roses, gathered for a vase,
In that chamber died apace,
Beam and breeze resigning –
This dog only, waited on,
Knowing that when light is gone,
Love remains for shining.

Other dogs in thymy dew
Tracked the hares and followed through
Sunny moor or meadow –
This dog only, crept and crept
Next a languid cheek that slept,
Sharing in the shadow.

Other dogs of loyal cheer
Bounded at the whistle clear,
Up the woodside hieing –
This dog only, watched in reach

Of a faintly uttered speech,
Or a louder sighing.

And if one or two quick tears
Dropped upon his glossy ears,
Or a sigh came double,
Up he sprang in eager haste,
Fawning, fondling, breathing fast,
In a tender trouble.

And this dog was satisfied,
If a pale thin hand would glide,
Down his dewlaps sloping, –
Which he pushed his nose within,
After, – platforming his chin
On the palm left open.

This dog, if a friendly voice
Call him now to blyther choice
Than such chamber-keeping,
Come out ! ' praying from the door, –
Presseth backward as before,
Up against me leaping.

Therefore to this dog will I,
Tenderly not scornfully,
Render praise and favour !
With my hand upon his head,
Is my benediction said
Therefore, and for ever.

And because he loves me so,
Better than his kind will do
Often, man or woman,
Give I back more love again
Than dogs often take of men, –
Leaning from my Human.

Blessings on thee, dog of mine,
Pretty collars make thee fine,
Sugared milk make fat thee !
Pleasures wag on in thy tail –
Hands of gentle motion fail
Nevermore, to pat thee !

Downy pillow take thy head,
Silken coverlid bestead,

Sunshine help thy sleeping !
No fly 's buzzing wake thee up –
No man break thy purple cup,
Set for drinking deep in.

Whiskered cats arointed flee –
Sturdy stoppers keep from thee
Cologne distillations ;
Nuts lie in thy path for stones,
And thy feast-day macaroons
Turn to daily rations!

Elizabeth Barrett Browning (1806–61)

A Flower in a Letter

My lonely chamber next the sea,
Is full of many flowers set free
By summer's earliest duty;
Dear friends upon the garden-walk
Might stop amid their fondest talk,
To pull the least in beauty.

A thousand flowers – each seeming one
That learnt, by gazing on the sun,
To counterfeit his shining –
Within whose leaves the holy dew
That falls from heaven, hath won anew
A glory...in declining.

Red roses used to praises long,
Contented with the poet's song,
The nightingale's being over :
And lilies white, prepared to touch
The whitest thought, nor soil it much,
Of dreamer turned to lover.

Deep violets you liken to
The kindest eyes that look on you,
Without a thought disloyal:
And cactuses, a queen might don,
If weary of her golden crown,
And still appear as royal!

Pansies for ladies all! I wis
That none who wear such brooches, miss
A jewel in the mirror:
And tulips, children love to stretch
Their fingers down, to feel in each
Its beauty's secret nearer.

Love's language may be talked with these!
To work out choicest sentences,
No blossoms can be meeter, –
And, such being used in Eastern bowers,
Young maids may wonder if the flowers
Or meanings be the sweeter.

And such being strewn before a bride,
Her little foot may turn aside,

Their longer bloom decreeing!
Unless some voices whispered sound
Should make her gaze upon the ground
Too earnestly – for seeing.

And such being scattered on a grave,
Whoever mourneth there may have
A type that seemeth worthy
Of a fair body hid below,
Which bloomed on earth a time ago,
Then perished as the earthy.

And such being wreathed for worldly feast,
Across the brimming cup some guest
Their rainbow colours viewing,
May feel them, – with a silent start, –
The covenant, his childish heart
With nature, made, – renewing.

No flowers our gardened England hath,
To match with these, in bloom and breath,
Which from the world are hiding
In sunny Devon moist with rills, –

A nunnery of cloistered hills, –
The elements presiding.

By Loddon's stream the flowers are fair
That meet one gifted lady's care
With prodigal rewarding ;
But Beauty is too used to run
To Mitford's bower – to want the sun
To light her through the garden!

And here, all summers are comprised-
The nightly frosts shrink exorcised
Before the priestly moonshine!
And every wind with stoled feet,
In wandering down the alleys sweet,
Steps lightly on the sunshine;

And (having promised Harpocrate
Among the nodding roses, that
No harm shall touch his daughters)
Gives quite away the noisy sound,
He dares not use upon such ground,
To ever-trickling waters.

Yet, sun and wind! what can ye do,
But make the leaves more brightly shew
In posies newly gathered? –
I look away from all your best;
To one poor flower unlike the rest, –
A little flower half- withered.

I do not think it ever was
A pretty flower, – to make the grass
Look greener where it reddened:
And now it seems ashamed to be
Alone in all this company,
Of aspect shrunk and saddened!

A chamber-window was the spot
It grew in, from a garden-pot,
Among the city shadows:
If any, tending it, might seem
To smile, 't was only in a dream
Of nature in the meadows.
How coldly, on its head, did fall
The sunshine, from the city wall,

In pale refraction driven!
How sadly plashed upon its leaves
The raindrops, losing in the eaves
The first sweet news of Heaven!

And those who planted, gathered it
In gamesome or in loving fit,
And sent it as a token
Of what their city pleasures be, –
For one, in Devon by the sea,
And garden-blooms, to look on.

But she, for whom the jest was meant,
With a grave passion innocent
Receiving what was given, –
Oh! if her face she turned then,
Let none say't was to gaze again
Upon the flowers of Devon!

Because, whatever virtue dwells
In genial skies – warm oracles
For gardens brightly springing, –

The flower which grew beneath your eyes,
Ah sweetest friends, to mine supplies
A beauty worthier singing!

Elizabeth Barrett Browning (1806–61)

EBBING AND FLOWING OF THE SEA

The reason the sea so constant Ebbs and Flowes,
Is like the Hammer of a Clocke, which goes.
For when it come just to the Notch, doth strike,
So water to that empty place doth like.
For when it Flowes, Water cast out still,
And when it Ebbs, runs back that place to fill.

Duchess of Newcastle Margaret Cavendish (1623–73)

A Song of Grief

Glazed silk, newly cut, smooth, glittering, white,

As white, as clear, even as frost and snow.

Perfectly fashioned into a fan,

Round, round, like the brilliant moon,

Treasured in my Lord's sleeve, taken out, put in—

Wave it, shake it, and a little wind flies from it.

How often I fear the Autumn Season's coming

And the fierce, cold wind which scatters the blazing heat.

Discarded, passed by, laid in a box alone;

Such a little time, and the thing of love cast off.

Pan Chieh-Yü (c. A.D. 400)

Dancing

Wide sleeves sway.

Scents,

Sweet scents

Incessantly coming.

It is red lilies,

Lotus lilies,

Floating up,

And up,

Out of Autumn mist.

Thin clouds

Puffed,

Fluttered,

Blown on a rippling wind

Through a mountain pass.

Young willow shoots

Touching,

Brushing,

The water

Of the garden pool.

Yang Kuei-Fei (A.D. 719–56)

LETTER TO J.G. WHITTIER

To J.G. Whittier
Norton, Mass., September 8, 1861

Why is it that I always miss thy visits? Why of all things should I have lost sight of thee at the mountains? and when I was so near thee too! I cannot think why so pleasant a thing should be withheld from me, unless because I enjoy it too much. I have no other such friends as thee and Elizabeth, and when anything like this happens it is a great disappointment. But I said all the time that seeing the hills with you could only be a beautiful dream.

I felt the beauty of those mountains around the Lake, as I floated among them, but I wished for thee all the while; because I have always associated thee with my first glimpse of them, and somehow it seems as if they belonged to thee or thee to them, or both. They would not speak to me much; I needed an interpreter: and when they grew so dim and spectral in the noon haze, they gave me a strange almost shuddering feeling of distance and loneliness.

But I am glad thee saw the Notch Mountains, and those grand blue hills up the river that I used to watch through all their changes. I am glad Miss B— saw thee, for she was as much disappointed as I when we gave up the hope of your coming. I felt almost certain you would both come; I wanted Lizzie to know the mountains.

Is it right to dream and plan for another year? How I should like to go to Franconia with thee and Elizabeth to see those great gates of the Notch open gradually wider and wider, and then to pass through to a vision of the vast range beyond! It is but a vague memory to me; I long to take that journey again.

But everything has wearied me this summer, and I feel almost like dropping my dreams and never expecting anything more. It is doubtless wiser to take what a kind Providence sends, just as it comes: yet who is always wise? Twice I rested in the sight of your beautiful river and on that cottage doorstep at Campton, looking off to the mountains. But the sea tired me with its restlessness. I wanted to tell it to be still. And I was very willing to get back from it to the quiet of my room, to the shelter of these friendly elms, and to the steady cheerful music of crickets and grasshoppers.

I shall be very happy to try to write a hymn for the Horticultural Association, as you request; and will send you something as soon as I can.

Lucy Larcom (1824–93)

THE TWO SHAKESPEARE TERCENTENARIES:
OF BIRTH, 1864: OF DEATH, 1916

To Shakespeare

Longer than thine, than thine,
Is now my time of life; and thus thy years
Seem to be clasped and harboured within mine.
O how ignoble this my clasp appears!

Thy unprophetic birth,
Thy darkling death: living I might have seen
That cradle, marked those labours, closed that earth.
O first, O last, O infinite between!

Now that my life has shared
Thy dedicated date, O mortal, twice,
To what all-vain embrace shall be compared
My lean enclosure of thy paradise?

To ignorant arms that fold
A poet to a foolish breast? The Line,
That is not, with the world within its hold?
So, days with days, my days encompass thine.
Child, Stripling, Man – the sod.

Might I talk little language to thee, pore
On thy last silence? O thou city of God,
My waste lies after thee, and lies before.

Alice Meynell (1847–1922)

EASTER NIGHT

All night had shout of men and cry
Of woeful women filled His way;
Until that noon of sombre sky
On Friday, clamour and display
Smote Him; no solitude had He,
No silence, since Gethsemane.

Public was Death; but Power, but Might,
But Life again, but Victory,
Were hushed within the dead of night,
The shutter'd dark, the secrecy.
And all alone, alone, alone
He rose again behind the stone.

Alice Meynell (1847–1922)

A Better Resurrection

I have no wit, no words, no tears;
My heart within me like a stone
Is numbed too much for hopes or fears;
Look right, look left, I dwell alone;
I lift mine eyes, but dimmed with grief
No everlasting hills I see;
My life is in the falling leaf:
O Jesus, quicken me!

My life is like a faded leaf,
My harvest dwindled to a husk;
Truly my life is void and brief
And tedious in the barren dusk;
My life is like a frozen thing,
No bud nor greenness can I see:
Yet rise it shall, – the sap of Spring;
O Jesus, rise in me!

My life is like a broken bowl,
A broken bowl that cannot hold
One drop of water for my soul

Or cordial in the searching cold;
Cast in the fire the perished thing,
Melt and remould it, till it be
A royal cup for Him my King:
O Jesus, drink of me!

Christina Rossetti (1830–94)

Art and Life

When Art goes bounding, lean,
Up hill-tops fired green
To pluck a rose for life.

Life like a broody hen
Cluck-clucks him back again.

But when Art, imbecile,
Sits old and chill
On sidings shaven clean,
And counts his clustering
Dead daisies on a string
With witless laughter....

Then like a new Jill
Toiling up a hill
Life scrambles after.

Lola Ridge (1873–1941)

MOONLIGHT

The stars around the fair moon fade
Against the night,
When gazing full she fills the glade
And spreads the seas with silvery light.

Sappho (b. 620 B.C.)

Song of the Rose

If Zeus chose us a King of the flowers in his mirth,
He would call to the rose, and would royally crown it;
For the rose, ho, the rose! is the grace of the earth,
Is the light of the plants that are growing upon it!
For the rose, ho, the rose! is the eye of the flowers,
Is the blush of the meadows that feel themselves fair,—
Is the lightning of beauty, that strikes through the bowers
On pale lovers that sit in the glow unaware.
Ho, the rose breathes of love! ho, the rose lifts the cup
To the red lips of Cypris invoked for a guest!
Ho, the rose having curled its sweet leaves for the world
Takes delight in the motion its petals keep up,
As they laugh to the Wind as it laughs from the west.

Sappho (b. 620 B.C.)

Untitled

Now the cherry trees seem to have bloomed;

it's cloudy,

hazy with spring

the way the world appears

Princess Shikishi (1149–1201)

The Prayer

'Many worlds have I made,' said the Good God,
'But this is best of all,'
He slipped the round earth from His lap,
Space held the circling ball.

'Six days have I laboured,' said the Good God,
'To make it very fair,
And man and woman have I moulded fine,
Set them together there.

'Open ye night's windows,' said the Good God,
'For I would hear them pray,'
Up from the spinning globe there came
Loud cries from far away.

'Into my hands deliver,' cried the man,
'The chast'ning of my foe,
His vineyards grant me—his slaves and oxen,
So shall I lay him low.'

'Give to me strange beauty,' said the young maid,
'More fair than all to be,
So I anoint my body and go forth
To draw men's hearts to me.'

'Behold! this is not good,' said the Lord God,
'Nor made to My desire,'
Then cried His little Son, 'I shall go forth,
To save them from Thine ire.'

*

'Oh, reach ye down your arms,' said the Good God
Unto the seraphim,
'Lift up the broken body of My child
For they have tortured Him.'

'Open the windows of the night,' said the Good God,
'For I would hear them weep,'
Up from the spinning world's tumultuous sound
Man's prayers imperious leap.

'Into my hands deliver,' cried the man,
'My foe to bend and break,
Burst Thou his strongholds and his ships entomb,
So I my vengeance take.'

'Give to me rare beauty,' said the young maid,
'More fair than all to be,
So I in silken raiment shall go forth
To draw men's souls to me.'

Dora Sigerson Shorter (1866–1918)

HAUNTED

How restless are the dead whose silent feet will stray
In to our lone retreat or solitary way;
Within the dew-wet wood or sun-enchanted lane
We meet them face to face, we hear them speak again.

How powerful are the dead whose voices ever speak,
So softly by our side in accents faint and weak:
They bid us go or stay, or do, or leave undone,
We hear them breathe our name ere dawn has well begun.

How silent are the dead when come accusing fears
To chide our aching hearts, to fill our days with tears:
They hush not now our grief, nor heed us as we plead
For some unspoken word, or some ungentle deed.

Beside the golden fire they take the empty chair
They tread from room to room, they pass from stair to stair,
And when comes tranquil night to call to us to sleep
Within our pleasant dreams the restless dead will creep.

How pitiless the dead who come in dearest guise
And most beloved ways before our wistful eyes;
To cry to us lost words that we remembered not,
To act again each scene that we had half forgot.

And should we seek to ease our heart with some caress
How timidly they fly and leave us loneliness:
How fugitive the dead who at our stricken call
Hide in the chilly tomb and answer not at all.

Dora Sigerson Shorter (1866–1918)

TRANSLATION

We trekked into a far country,
My friend and I.
Our deeper content was never spoken,
But each knew all the other said.
He told me how calm his soul was laid
By the lack of anvil and strife.
'The wooing kestrel,' I said, 'mutes his mating-note
To please the harmony of this sweet silence.'
And when at the day's end
We laid tired bodies 'gainst
The loose warm sands,
And the air fleeced its particles for a coverlet;
When star after star came out
To guard their lovers in oblivion –
My soul so leapt that my evening prayer
Stole my morning song!

Anne Spencer (1882–1975)

CLIMBING A MOUNTAIN

High rises the Eastern Peak
Soaring up to the blue sky.
Among the rocks – an empty hollow,
Secret, still, mysterious!
Uncarved and unhewn,
Screened by nature with a roof of clouds.
Times and Seasons, what things are you
Bringing to my life ceaseless change?
I will lodge for ever in this hollow
Where Springs and Autumns unheeded pass.

Tao-yün (c. A.D. 400)

ON VIRTUE

O Thou bright jewel in my aim I strive
To comprehend thee. Thine own words declare
Wisdom is higher than a fool can reach.
I cease to wonder, and no more attempt
Thine height t' explore, or fathom thy profound.

But, O my soul, sink not into despair,
Virtue is near thee, and with gentle hand
Would now embrace thee, hovers o'er thine head.
Fain would the heav'n-born soul with her converse,
Then seek, then court her for her promis'd bliss.
Auspicious queen, thine heav'nly pinions spread,
And lead celestial Chastity along;

Lo! now her sacred retinue descends,
Array'd in glory from the orbs above.
Attend me, Virtue, thro' my youthful years!
O leave me not to the false joys of time!
But guide my steps to endless life and bliss.

Greatness, or Goodness, say what I shall call thee,

To give me an higher appellation still,

Teach me a better strain, a nobler lay,

O thou, enthron'd with Cherubs in the realms of day.

Phillis Wheatley (c. 1753–84)

On Imagination

Thy various works, imperial queen, we see,
How bright their forms! how deck'd with pomp
   by thee!
Thy wond'rous acts in beauteous order stand,
And all attest how potent is thine hand.
From Helicon's refulgent heights attend,
Ye sacred choir, and my attempts befriend:
To tell her glories with a faithful tongue,
Ye blooming graces, triumph in my song.
 Now here, now there, the roving Fancy flies,
Till some lov'd object strikes her wand'ring eyes,
Whose silken fetters all the senses bind,
And soft captivity involves the mind.
Imagination! who can sing thy force?
Or who describe the swiftness of thy course?
Soaring through air to find the bright abode,
Th' empyreal palace of the thund'ring God,
We on thy pinions can surpass the wind,
And leave the rolling universe behind:
From star to star the mental optics rove,
Measure the skies, and range the realms above.

There in one view we grasp the mighty whole,
Or with new worlds amaze th' unbounded soul.
Though Winter frowns to Fancy's raptur'd eyes
The fields may flourish, and gay scenes arise;
The frozen deeps may break their iron bands,
And bid their waters murmur o'er the sands.
Fair Flora may resume her fragrant reign,
And with her flow'ry riches deck the plain;
Sylvanus may diffuse his honours round,
And all the forest may with leaves be crown'd:
Show'rs may descend, and dews their gems disclose,
And nectar sparkle on the blooming rose.
Such is thy pow'r, nor are thine orders vain,
O thou the leader of the mental train:
In full perfection all thy works are wrought,
And thine the sceptre o'er the realms of thought.
Before thy throne the subject-passions bow,
Of subject-passions sov'reign ruler thou;
At thy command joy rushes on the heart,
And through the glowing veins the spirits dart.
Fancy might now her silken pinions try
To rise from earth, and sweep th' expanse on high:
From Tithon's bed now might Aurora rise,
Her cheeks all glowing with celestial dies,

While a pure stream of light o'erflows the skies.
The monarch of the day I might behold,
And all the mountains tipt with radiant gold,
But I reluctant leave the pleasing views,
Which Fancy dresses to delight the Muse;
Winter austere forbids me to aspire,
And northern tempests damp the rising fire;
They chill the tides of Fancy's flowing sea,
Cease then, my song, cease the unequal lay.

Phillis Wheatley (c. 1753–84)

A Place
and Time in
the World

LINES WRITTEN ABROAD

I have but left my pleasant home
And native vales, to die!
Ah wherefore did the wish to roam,
So wildly o'er my spirit come,
And urge so temptingly!

My Mother! – thou wilt hope in vain,
Thy wandering one's return:
'Twould calm the bitterness of pain,
If once on thy dear face again
My parting glance might turn.

But sever'd thus by land, and wave,
From tenderness, and thee,
And all whose love, might sooth, or save,
I perish here-and ev'n my grave
In stranger-earth must be!

Eliza Acton (1799–1859)

The Ballad Which Anne Askew Made and Sang When She Was in Newgate

Like as the armed knight
Appointed to the field,
With this world will I fight
And Faith shall be my shield.

Faith is that weapon strong
Which will not fail at need.
My foes, therefore, among
Therewith will I proceed.

As it is had in strength
And force of Christes way
It will prevail at length
Though all the devils say nay.

Faith in the fathers old
Obtained rightwisness
Which make me very bold
To fear no world's distress.

I now rejoice in heart

And Hope bid me do so

For Christ will take my part

And ease me of my woe.

Thou saist, lord, who so knock,

To them wilt thou attend.

Undo, therefore, the lock

And thy strong power send.

More enmyes now I have

Than hairs upon my head.

Let them not me deprave

But fight thou in my stead.

On thee my care I cast.

For all their cruel spight

I set not by their haste

For thou art my delight.

I am not she that list
My anchor to let fall
For every drizzling mist
My ship substancial.

Not oft use I to wright
In prose nor yet in rime,
Yet will I shew one sight
That I saw in my time.

I saw a rial throne
Where Justice should have sit
But in her stead was one
Of moody cruel wit.

Absorpt was rightwisness
As of the raging flood
Sathan in his excess
Suct up the guiltless blood.

Then thought I, Jesus lord,
When thou shalt judge us all
Hard is it to record

On these men what will fall.

Yet lord, I thee desire
For that they do to me
Let them not taste the hire
Of their iniquity.

Anne Askew (1521–46)

LAMENT OF HSI-CHÜN

My people have married me
In a far corner of Earth:
Sent me away to a strange land,
To the king of the Wu-sun.
A tent is my house,
Of felt are my walls;
Raw flesh my food
With mare's milk to drink.
Always thinking of my own country,
My heart sad within.
Would I were a yellow stork
And could fly to my old home!

Hsi-Chun (c. 110 B.C.)

Setting Sail

Exultation is the going
Of an inland soul to sea, –
Past the houses, past the headlands,
Into deep eternity!

Bred as we, among the mountains,
Can the sailor understand
The divine intoxication
Of the first league out from land?

Emily Dickinson (1830–86)

God Bless Our Native Land

God bless our native land,
Land of the newly free,
Oh may she ever stand
For truth and liberty.

God bless our native land,
Where sleep our kindred dead,
Let peace at thy command
Above their graves be shed.

God help our native land,
Bring surcease to her strife,
And shower from thy hand
A more abundant life.

God bless our native land,
Her homes and children bless,
Oh may she ever stand
For truth and righteousness.

Frances Harper (1825–1911)

New York at Night

A near horizon whose sharp jags
Cut brutally into a sky
Of leaden heaviness, and crags
Of houses lift their masonry
Ugly and foul, and chimneys lie
And snort, outlined against the gray
Of lowhung cloud. I hear the sigh
The goaded city gives, not day
Nor night can ease her heart, her anguished labours stay.

Below, straight streets, monotonous,
From north and south, from east and west,
Stretch glittering; and luminous
Above, one tower tops the rest
And holds aloft man's constant quest:
Time! Joyless emblem of the greed
Of millions, robber of the best
Which earth can give, the vulgar creed
Has seared upon the night its flaming ruthless screed.

O Night! Whose soothing presence brings
The quiet shining of the stars.
O Night! Whose cloak of darkness clings
So intimately close that scars
Are hid from our own eyes. Beggars
By day, our wealth is having night
To burn our souls before altars
Dim and tree-shadowed, where the light
Is shed from a young moon, mysteriously bright.

Where art thou hiding, where thy peace?
This is the hour, but thou art not.
Will waking tumult never cease?
Hast thou thy votary forgot?
Nature forsakes this man-begot
And festering wilderness, and now
The long still hours are here, no jot
Of dear communing do I know;
Instead the glaring, man-filled city groans below!

Amy Lowell (1874–1925)

THE ROAD TO AVIGNON

A Minstrel stands on a marble stair,
Blown by the bright wind, debonair;
Below lies the sea, a sapphire floor,
Above on the terrace a turret door
Frames a lady, listless and wan,
But fair for the eye to rest upon.
The minstrel plucks at his silver strings,
And looking up to the lady, sings: –
    Down the road to Avignon,
    The long, long road to Avignon,
    Across the bridge to Avignon,
    One morning in the spring.

The octagon tower casts a shade
Cool and gray like a cutlass blade;
In sun-baked vines the cicalas spin,
The little green lizards run out and in.
A sail dips over the ocean's rim,
And bubbles rise to the fountain's brim.
The minstrel touches his silver strings,
And gazing up to the lady, sings: –
    Down the road to Avignon,

The long, long road to Avignon,
Across the bridge to Avignon,
One morning in the spring.

Slowly she walks to the balustrade,
Idly notes how the blossoms fade
In the sun's caress; then crosses where
The shadow shelters a carven chair.
Within its curve, supine she lies,
And wearily closes her tired eyes.
The minstrel beseeches his silver strings,
And holding the lady spellbound, sings: –
Down the road to Avignon,
The long, long road to Avignon,
Across the bridge to Avignon,
One morning in the spring.

Clouds sail over the distant trees,
Petals are shaken down by the breeze,
They fall on the terrace tiles like snow;
The sighing of waves sounds, far below.
A humming-bird kisses the lips of a rose
Then laden with honey and love he goes.
The minstrel woos with his silver strings,

And climbing up to the lady, sings: –
Down the road to Avignon,
The long, long road to Avignon,
Across the bridge to Avignon,
One morning in the spring.

Step by step, and he comes to her,
Fearful lest she suddenly stir.
Sunshine and silence, and each to each,
The lute and his singing their only speech;
He leans above her, her eyes unclose,
The humming-bird enters another rose.
The minstrel hushes his silver strings.
Hark! The beating of humming-birds' wings!
Down the road to Avignon,
The long, long road to Avignon,
Across the bridge to Avignon,
One morning in the spring.

Amy Lowell (1874–1925)

A London Thoroughfare at 2 A.M.

They have watered the street,
It shines in the glare of lamps,
Cold, white lamps,
And lies
Like a slow-moving river,
Barred with silver and black.
Cabs go down it,
One,
And then another.
Between them I hear the shuffling of feet.
Tramps doze on the window-ledges,
Night-walkers pass along the sidewalks.
The city is squalid and sinister,
With the silver-barred street in the midst,
Slow-moving,
A river leading nowhere.

Opposite my window,
The moon cuts,
Clear and round,
Through the plum-coloured night.

She cannot light the city;
It is too bright.
It has white lamps,
And glitters coldly.

I stand in the window and watch the moon.
She is thin and lustreless,
But I love her.
I know the moon,
And this is an alien city.

Amy Lowell (1874–1925)

Summer in England, 1914

On London fell a clearer light;
Caressing pencils of the sun
Defined the distances, the white
Houses transfigured one by one,
The 'long, unlovely street' impearled.
O what a sky has walked the world!

Most happy year! And out of town
The hay was prosperous, and the wheat;
The silken harvest climbed the down;
Moon after moon was heavenly-sweet
Stroking the bread within the sheaves,
Looking twixt apples and their leaves.

And while this rose made round her cup,
The armies died convulsed. And when
This chaste young silver sun went up
Softly, a thousand shattered men,
One wet corruption, heaped the plain,
After a league-long throb of pain.

Flower following tender flower; and birds,
And berries; and benignant skies
Made thrive the serried flocks and herds.
Yonder are men shot through the eyes.
Love, hide thy face
From man's unpardonable race.

*

Who said 'No man hath greater love than this,
To die to serve his friend?'
So these have loved us all unto the end.
Chide thou no more, O thou unsacrificed!
The soldier dying dies upon a kiss,
The very kiss of Christ.

Alice Meynell (1847–1922)

LENGTH OF DAYS

To the early dead in battle

There is no length of days
But yours, boys who were children once. Of old
The past beset you in your childish ways,
With sense of Time untold!

What have you then forgone?
A history? This you had. Or memories?
These, too, you had of your far-distant dawn.
No further dawn seems his,

The old man who shares with you,
But has no more, no more. Time's mystery
Did once for him the most that it can do:
He has had infancy.

And all his dreams, and all
His loves for mighty Nature, sweet and few,
Are but the dwindling past he can recall
Of what his childhood knew.

He counts not any more
His brief, his present years. But O he knows
How far apart the summers were of yore,
How far apart the snows.

Therefore be satisfied;
Long life is in your treasury ere you fall;
Yes, and first love, like Dante's. O a bride
For ever mystical!

Irrevocable good,–
You dead, and now about, so young, to die,–
Your childhood was; there Space, there Multitude,
There dwelt Antiquity.

Alice Meynell (1847–1922)

A Wind of Clear Weather in England

O what a miracle wind is this
Has crossed the English land to-day
With an unprecedented kiss,
And wonderfully found a way!

Unsmirched incredibly and clean,
Between the towns and factories,
Avoiding, has his long flight been,
Bringing a sky like Sicily's.

O fine escape, horizon pure
As Rome's! Black chimneys left and right,
But not for him, the straight, the sure,
His luminous day, his spacious night.

How keen his choice, how swift his feet!
Narrow the way and hard to find!
This delicate stepper and discreet
Walked not like any worldly wind.

Most like a man in man's own day,
One of the few, a perfect one:
His open earth – the single way;
His narrow road – the open sun.

Alice Meynell (1847–1922)

At Bay St Louis

Soft breezes blow and swiftly show
Through fragrant orange branches parted,
A maiden fair, with sun-flecked hair,
Caressed by arrows, golden darted.
The vine-clad tree holds forth to me
A promise sweet of purple blooms,
And chirping bird, scarce seen but heard
Sings dreamily, and sweetly croons
At Bay St. Louis.

The hammock swinging, idly singing,
Lissome nut-brown maid
Swings gaily, freely, to-and-fro;
The curling, green-white waters casting cool, clear shade,
Rock small, shell boats that go
In circles wide, or tug at anchor's chain,
As though to skim the sea with cargo vain,
At Bay St. Louis.

The maid swings slower, slower to-and-fro,
And sunbeams kiss gray, dreamy half-closed eyes;
Fond lover creeping on with foot steps slow,
Gives gentle kiss, and smiles at sweet surprise.

The lengthening shadows tell that eve is nigh,
And fragrant zephyrs cool and calmer grow,
Yet still the lover lingers, and scarce breathed sigh,
Bids the swift hours to pause, nor go,
At Bay St. Louis.

Alice Moore-Dunbar Nelson (1875–1935)

MANHATTAN

Out of the night you burn, Manhattan,
In a vesture of gold –
Span of innumerable arcs,
Flaring and multiplying –
Gold at the uttermost circles fading
Into the tenderest hint of jade,
Or fusing in tremulous twilight blues,
Robing the far-flung offices,
Scintillant-storied, forking flame,
Or soaring to luminous amethyst
Over the steeples aureoled –

Diaphanous gold,
Veiling the Woolworth, argently
Rising slender and stark
Mellifluous-shrill as a vender's cry,
And towers squatting graven and cold
On the velvet bales of the dark,
And the Singer's appraising
Indolent idol's eye,
And night like a purple cloth unrolled –

Nebulous gold

Throwing an ephemeral glory about life's vanishing points,

Wherein you burn…

You of unknown voltage

Whirling on your axis…

Scrawling vermillion signatures

Over the night's velvet hoarding…

Insolent, towering spherical

To apices ever shifting.

Lola Ridge (1873–1941)

THE SLEEP WIND

Softer than mists o'er the pale green of waters,
O'er the charmed sea, shod with sandals of shadow
Comes the warm sleep wind of Argolis, floating
Garlands of fragrance;

Comes the sweet wind by the still hours attended,
Touching tired lids on the shores dim with distance,
Ever its way toward the headland of Lesbos,
Toward Mitylene.

Faintly one fair star of evening enkindles
On the dusk afar its lone fire Œtean,
Shining serene till the darkness will deepen
Others to splendor;

Bringing ineffable peace, and the gladsome
Return with the night of all things that morning
Ruthlessly parted, the child to its mother,
Lover to lover.

From the marble court of rose-crowned companions,
All alone my feet again seek the little

Theatre pledged to the Muse, now deserted,
Facing the surges;

Where the carved Pan-heads that laugh down the gentle
Slope of broad steps to the refluent ripple,
Flute from their thin pipes the dithyrambs deathless,
Songs all unuttered.

Empty each seat where my girl friends acclaimed me,
Poets with names on the tiered stone engraven,
Over whose verge blooms the apple tree, drifting
Perfume and petals;

Gone Telesippa and tender Gyrinno,
Anactoria, woman divine; Atthis,
Subtlest of soul, fair Damophyla, Dica,
Maids of the Muses.

Here an hour past soul-enravished they listened
While my rapt heart breathed its pæan impassioned,
Chanted its wild prayer to thee, Aphrodite,
Daughter of Cyprus;

Now to their homes are they gone in the city,
Pensive to dream limb-relaxed while the languid
Slaves come and lift from the tresses they loosen,
Flowers that have faded.

Thou alone, Sappho, art sole with the silence,
Sole with night and dreams that are darkness, weaving
Thoughts that are sighs from the heart and their meaning
Vague as the shadow;

When the great silence shall come to thee, sad one,
Men that forget shall remember thy music,
Murmur thy name that shall steal on their passion
Soft as the sleep wind.

Sappho (b. 620 B.C.)

UNTITLED

The kind of place
where the way a traveller's tracks
disappear in snow
is something you get used to –
such a place is this world of ours.

Princess Shikishi (1149–1201)

The Road of the Refugees

Listen to the tramping! Oh, God of pity, listen!
Can we kneel at prayer, sleep all unmolested,
While the echo thunders? – God of pity, listen!
Can we think of prayer – or sleep – so arrested?

Million upon million fleeing feet in passing
Trample down our prayers – trample down our sleeping;
How the patient roads groan beneath the massing
Of the feet in going, bleeding, running, creeping!

Clank of iron shoe, unshod hooves of cattle,
Pad of roaming hound, creak of wheel in turning,
Clank of dragging chain, harness ring and rattle,
Groan of breaking beam, crash of roof-tree burning.

Listen to the tramping! – God of love and pity!
Million upon million fleeing feet in passing
Driven by the war out of field and city,
How the sullen road echoes to the massing!

Little feet of children, running, leaping, lagging,
Toiling feet of women, wounded, weary guiding,
Slow feet of the aged, stumbling, halting, flagging,
Strong feet of the men loud in passion striding.

Hear the lost feet straying, from the roadway slipping,
They will walk no longer in this march appalling;
Hear the sound of rain dripping, dripping, dripping,
Is it rain or tears? What, O God, is falling?

Hear the flying feet! Lord of love and pity!
Crushing down our prayers, tramping down our sleeping,
Driven by the war out of field and city,
Million upon million, running, bleeding, creeping.

Dora Sigerson Shorter (1866–1918)

Impressions in Belgium

September 25th, 1914

And we have landed at Ostend.

I'll confess now that I dreaded Ostend more than anything. We had been told that there were horrors upon horrors in Ostend. Children were being born in the streets, and the state of the bathing-machines where the refugees lived was unspeakable. I imagined the streets of Ostend crowded with refugee women bearing children, and the Digue covered with the horrific bathing-machines. On the other hand, Ostend was said to be the safest spot in Europe. No Germans there. No Zeppelins. No bombs.

And we found the bathing-machines planted out several miles from the town, almost invisible specks on a vanishing shore-line. The refugees we met walking about the streets of Ostend were in fairly good case and bore themselves bravely. But the town had been bombarded the night before and our hotel had been the object of very special attentions. We chose it (the 'Terminus') because it lay close to the landing-stage and saved us the trouble of going into the town to look for quarters. It was under the same roof as the railway station, where we proposed to leave our ambulance cars and heavy luggage. And we had no difficulty whatever in getting rooms for the whole thirteen of us. There was no sort of competition for rooms in that hotel. I said to myself, 'If Ostend ever is bombarded, this railway station will be the first to suffer. And the hotel and the railway station are one.' And when I was shown into a bedroom with glass windows all along its inner wall and a fine glass front looking out on to the platforms under the immense glass roof of the station, I said, 'If this hotel is ever bombarded, what fun it will be for the person who sleeps in this bed between these glass windows.'

We were all rather tired and hungry as we met for dinner at seven o'clock. And when we were told that all lights would be put out in the town at eight-thirty we only thought that a municipality which was receiving all the refugees in Belgium must practise *some* economy, and that, anyway, an hour and a half was enough for anybody to dine in; and we hoped that the Commandant, who had gone to call on the English chaplain at the Grand Hôtel Littoral, would find his way back again to the peaceful and commodious shelter of the 'Terminus.'

He did find his way back, at seven-thirty, just in time to give us a chance of clearing out, if we chose to take it. The English chaplain, it seemed, was surprised and dismayed at our idea of a suitable hotel, and he implored us to fly, instantly, before a bomb burst in among us (this was the first we had heard of the bombardment of the night before). The Commandant put it to us as we sat there: Whether would we leave that dining-room at once and pack our baggage all over again, and bundle out, and go hunting for rooms all through Ostend with the lights out, and perhaps fall into the harbour; or stay where we were and risk the off-chance of a bomb? And we were all very tired and hungry, and we had only got to the soup, and we had seen (and smelt) the harbour, so we said we'd stay where we were and risk it.

And we stayed. A Taube hovered over us and never dropped its bomb.

May Sinclair (1863–1946)

DEDICATION

To a Field Ambulance in Flanders
I do not call you comrades,
You,
Who did what I only dreamed.
Though you have taken my dream,
And dressed yourselves in its beauty and its glory,
Your faces are turned aside as you pass by.
I am nothing to you,
For I have done no more than dream.

Your faces are like the face of her whom you follow,
Danger,
The Beloved who looks backward as she runs, calling
    to her lovers,
The Huntress who flies before her quarry, trailing her lure.
She called to me from her battle-places,
She flung before me the curved lightning of
    her shells for a lure;
And when I came within sight of her,
She turned aside,
And hid her face from me.

But you she loved;

You she touched with her hand;

For you the white flames of her feet stayed in their running;

She kept you with her in her fields of Flanders,

Where you go,

Gathering your wounded from among her dead.

Grey night falls on your going and black night on your
returning.

You go

Under the thunder of the guns, the shrapnel's rain and the
curved lightning of the shells,

And where the high towers are broken,

And houses crack like the staves of a thin crate filled
with fire;

Into the mixing smoke and dust of roof and walls
torn asunder

You go;

And only my dream follows you.

That is why I do not speak of you,

Calling you by your names.

Your names are strung with the names of ruined and
immortal cities,

Termonde and Antwerp, Dixmude and Ypres and Furnes,

Like jewels on one chain –
Thus,
In the high places of Heaven,
They shall tell all your names.
May Sinclair.

March 8th, 1915.

May Sinclair (1863–1946)

BELGIUM

La Belgique ne regrette rien
Not with her ruined silver spires,
Not with her cities shamed and rent,
Perish the imperishable fires
That shape the homestead from the tent.

Wherever men are staunch and free,
There shall she keep her fearless state,
And homeless, to great nations be
The home of all that makes them great.

Edith Wharton (1862–1937)

On Mrs. W—'s Voyage to England

I.

While raging tempests shake the shore,

While Ae'lus' thunders round us roar,

And sweep impetuous o'er the plain

Be still, O tyrant of the main;

Nor let thy brow contracted frowns betray,

While my Susanna skims the wat'ry way.

II.

The Pow'r propitious hears the lay,

The blue-ey'd daughters of the sea

With sweeter cadence glide along,

And Thames responsive joins the song.

Pleas'd with their notes Sol sheds benign his ray,

And double radiance decks the face of day.

III.

To court thee to Britannia's arms

Serene the climes and mild the sky,

Her region boasts unnumber'd charms,

Thy welcome smiles in ev'ry eye.

Thy promise, Neptune keep, record my pray'r,
Not give my wishes to the empty air.

Phillis Wheatley (c. 1753–84)

ON BEING BROUGHT FROM AFRICA TO AMERICA

'Twas mercy brought me from my Pagan land,
Taught my benighted soul to understand
That there's a God, that there's a Saviour too:
Once I redemption neither fought nor knew,
Some view our sable race with scornful eye,
'Their colour is a diabolic die.'
Remember, Christians, Negroes, black as Cain,
May be refin'd, and join th' angelic train.

Phillis Wheatley (c. 1753–84)

LOVE AND DESIRE

To ~

How sacred is the lightest thing
Which wakes a thought of thee!
The wild-flow'r's lonely blossoming;
The young spring-zephyr's laden wing,
Are spells, which to my bosom bring
Rich tides of memory!

Soft tones of music floating far
At ev'ning o'er the sea;
The trembling of the twilight star,
When not a cloud hath dar'd to mar
Its dewy smiles, – but sweet dreams are
Which lead my soul to thee!

Eliza Acton (1799–1859)

Sonnets d'Amour 6

Whoever claims that absence cures Love's sting
Has never felt that god's might, poised therefor:
Witness my woe, growing apace, the more
I quit the object of my suffering.

My spirit, in your presence reveling,
Cares for your love alone; and I, heartsore,
Forge endless love from your perfections' store,
Born, ever fresh, of my remembering.

When, close to mine, I see your love-illed eyes
And hear your words that I do so dearly proze,
I swoon, and, lovesick, lose all quickening.

But distant, now, constant and comfortless,
I see my love in all its langourousness:
And keener still, my pain, my anguishing.

Madeleine de l'Aubespine (1546–96)

Sonnets d'Amour 3

Let the earth cease its turning, suddenly,
And the fixed stars travel the firmament;
Let somber Saturn shine, benevolent;
Jupiter rule the hosts beneath the sea;

Let Mars turn peaceful; Sun's lush clarity
Turn dim, then dark; grown motionless, outspent;
Venus, unloving; Mercury, content,
Changeless; Monn square, no more circle be;

Let fire weigh heavy and the earth weigh light;
Water feel dry and warm; and let the flight
Of fish go coursing, grazing through the sky,

Sooner than might another know my love.
Born was I but to grant you all thereof:
For you alone I live, and for you, die.

Madeleine de l'Aubespine (1546–96)

Sonnet 43

How do I love thee? Let me count the ways.
I love thee to the depth and breadth and height
My soul can reach, when feeling out of sight
For the ends of Being and ideal Grace.
I love thee to the level of everyday's
Most quiet need, by sun and candlelight.
I love thee freely, as men strive for Right;
I love thee purely, as they turn from Praise.
I love thee with the passion put to use
In my old griefs, and with my childhood's faith.
I love thee with a love I seemed to lose
With my lost saints, – I love thee with the breath,
Smiles, tears, of all my life! – and, if God choose,
I shall but love thee better after death.

Elizabeth Barrett Browning (1806–61)

LETTER TO DAVID LEE CHILD

Phillips Beach, Sunday evening, August 8, 1830

Dearest Husband, – Here I am in a snug little old-fashioned parlor, at a round table, in a rocking-chair, writing to you, and the greatest comfort I have is the pen-knife you sharpened for me just before I came away. As you tell me sometimes, it makes my heart leap to see anything you have touched. The house here is real old-fashioned, neat, comfortable, rural, and quiet. There is a homespun striped carpet upon the floor, two profiles over the mantle-piece, one of them a soldier placed in a frame rather one-sided, with a white shirt ruffle, a white plume, and a white epaulette; a vase of flowers done in water colors, looking sickly and straggling about as if they were only neighbors-in-law, and Ophelia with a quantity of 'carrotty' hair, which is thrown over three or four rheumatic trees, and one foot ankle deep in water, as if she were going to see which she liked best, hanging or drowning.

These, with an old-fashioned table and desk, form a schedule of the furniture. The old lady is just like your good mother, just such honest shoulders, just such motions, a face very much like hers, and precisely the same kind motherly ways. I am sure you would be struck with the resemblance.

I like the whole family extremely. They are among the best specimens of New England farmers, as simple and as kind as little children. The food is excellent…. In the stillness of the evening we can hear the sea dashing on the beach, 'rolling its eternal bass' amid the harmony of nature. I went down to a little cove between two lines of rocks this morning, and having taken off my stockings, I let the saucy waves come dashing and sparkling into my lap. I was a little sad, because it made me think of the beautiful time we had, when we washed our feet together in the mountain waterfall. How I do wish you were here! It is nonsense for me to go a 'pleasuring' without you. It does me no good, and every pleasant sight makes my heart yearn for you to be with me. I am very homesick for you; and my private opinion is, that I shall not be able to stand it a whole week. As for the place itself, it is exactly what I wanted to find. Oh, how I do wish we had a snug little cottage here, and just income enough to meet very moderate wants. I have walked about a mile today, and got well mudded by plunging into a meadow after that brightest of all bright blossoms, the cardinal flower. My dear husband, I cannot stay away a week.

Lydia Maria Child (1802–80)

MARRIED LOVE

You and I
Have so much love,
That it
Burns like a fire,
In which we bake a lump of clay
Molded into a figure of you
And a figure of me.
Then we take both of them,
And break them into pieces,
And mix the pieces with water,
And mold again a figure of you,
And a figure of me.
I am in your clay.
In life we share a single quilt.
In death we will share a single coffin.

Guan Daosheng (1262–1319)

If You Were Coming in the Fall

If you were coming in the fall,
I'd brush the summer by
With half a smile and half a spurn,
As housewives do a fly.

If I could see you in a year,
I'd wind the months in balls,
And put them each in separate drawers,
Until their time befalls.

If only centuries delayed,
I'd count them on my hand,
Subtracting till my fingers dropped
Into Van Diemen's land.

If certain, when this life was out
That yours and mine should be,
I'd toss it yonder like a rind,
And taste eternity.

But now, all ignorant of the length

Of time's uncertain wing,

It goads me, like the goblin bee,

That will not state its sting.

Emily Dickinson (1830–86)

Renunciation

There came a day at summer's full
Entirely for me;
I thought that such were for the saints,
Where revelations be.

The sun, as common, went abroad,
The flowers, accustomed, blew,
As if no soul the solstice passed
That maketh all things new.

The time was scarce profaned by speech;
The symbol of a word
Was needless, as at sacrament
The wardrobe of our Lord.

Each was to each the sealed church,
Permitted to commune this time,
Lest we too awkward show
At supper of the Lamb.

The hours slid fast, as hours will,
Clutched tight by greedy hands;
So faces on two decks look back,
Bound to opposing lands.

And so, when all the time had failed,
Without external sound,
Each bound the other's crucifix,
We gave no other bond.

Sufficient troth that we shall rise
Deposed, at length, the grave –
To that new marriage, justified
Through Calvaries of Love!

Emily Dickinson (1830–86)

THE COMPLAINT OF A LOVER

Seest thou younder craggy Rock,
Whose Head o'er-looks the swelling Main,
Where never Shepherd fed his Flock,
Or careful Peasant sow'd his Grain.

No wholesome Herb grows on the same,
Or Bird of Day will on it rest;
'Tis Barren as the Hopeless Flame,
That scortches my tormented Breast.

Deep underneath a Cave does lie,
Th'entrance hid with dismal Yew,
Where *Phebus* never shew'd his Eye,
Or cheerful Day yet pierced through.

In that dark Melancholy Cell,
(Retreate and Sollace to my Woe)
Love, sad Dispair, and I, do dwell,
The Springs from whence my Griefs do flow.

Treacherous Love that did appear,
(When he at first approach't my Heart)
Drest in a Garb far from severe,
Or threatning ought of future smart.

So Innocent those Charms then seem'd,
When *Rosalinda* first I spy'd,
Ah! Who would them have deadly deem'd?
But Flowrs do often Serpents hide.

Beneath those sweets conceal'd lay,
To Love the cruel Foe, Disdain,
With which (alas) she does repay
My Constant and Deserving Pain.

When I in Tears have spent the Night,
With Sighs I usher in the Sun,
Who never saw a sadder sight,
In all the Courses he has run.

Sleep, which to others Ease does prove,
Comes unto me, alas, in vain:
For in my Dreams I am in Love,
And in them too she does Disdain.

Some times t'Amuse my Sorrow, I
Unto the hollow Rocks repair,
And loudly to the *Eccho* cry, Ah!
gentle Nimph come ease my Care.

Thou who, times past, a Lover wer't,
Ah! pity me, who now am so,
And by a sense of thine own smart,
Alleviate my Mighty Woe.

Come Flatter then, or Chide my Grief;
Catch my last Words, and call me Fool;
Or say, she Loves, for my Relief;
My Passion either sooth, or School.

Anne Killigrew (1660–85)

LOVE, THE SOUL OF POETRY

When first *Alexis* did in Verse delight,
His Muse in Low, but Graceful Numbers walk't,
And now and then a little Proudly stalk't;
But never aim'd at any noble Flight:
The Herds, the Groves, the gentle purling Streams,
Adorn'd his Song, and were his highest Theams.

But Love these Thoughts, like Mists, did soon disperse,
Enlarg'd his Fancy, and set free his Muse,
Biding him more Illustrious Subjects choose;
The Acts of Gods, and God-like Men reherse.
From thence new Raptures did his Breast inspire,
His scarce Warm-Heart converted was to Fire.

Th' exalted Poet rais'd by this new Flame,
With Vigor flys, where late he crept along,
And Acts Divine, in a Diviner Song,
Commits to the eternal Trompe of Fame.
And thus *Alexis* does prove Love to be,
As the Worlds Soul, the Soul of Poetry.

Anne Killigrew (1660–85)

To My Excellent Lucasia,
On Our Friendship

I did not live until this time
Crowned my felicity,
When I could say without a crime,
I am not thine, but thee.

This carcass breathed, and walked, and slept,
So that the world believed
There was a soul the motions kept;
But they were all deceived.

For as a watch by art is wound
To motion, such was mine:
But never had Orinda found
A soul till she found thine;

Which now inspires, cures and supplies,
And guides my darkened breast:
For thou art all that I can prize,
My joy, my life, my rest.

No bridegroom's nor crown-conqueror's mirth
To mine compared can be:
They have but pieces of the earth,
I've all the world in thee.

Then let our flames still light and shine,
And no false fear control,
As innocent as our design,
Immortal as our soul.

Katherine Philips (1632–64)

HYMN TO VENUS

Immortal Venus, throned above
In radiant beauty, child of Jove,
skilled in every art of love
And artful snare;
Dread power, to whom I bend the knee,
Release my soul and set it free
From bonds of piercing agony
And gloomy care.
Yet come thyself, if e'er, benign,
Thy listening ears thou didst incline
To my rude lay, the starry shine
Of Jove's court leaving,
In chariot yoked with coursers fair,
Thine own immortal birds that bear
Thee swift to earth, the middle air
With bright wings cleaving.
Soon they were sped – and thou, most blest,
In thine own smiles ambrosial dressed,
Didst ask what griefs my mind oppressed –
What meant my song –
What end my frenzied thoughts pursue –

For what loved youth I spread anew
My amorous nets – 'Who, Sappho, who
Hath done thee wrong?
What though he fly, he'll soon return –
Still press thy gifts, though now he spurn;
Heed not his coldness – soon he'll burn,
E'en though thou chide.'
 – And saidst thou thus, dread goddess? O,
Come then once more to ease my woe;
Grant all, and thy great self bestow,
My shield and guide!

Sappho (b. 620 B.C.)

The Daughter of Cyprus

Dreaming I spake with the Daughter of Cyprus,
Heard the languor soft of her voice, the blended
Suave accord of tones interfused with laughter
Low and desireful;

Dreaming saw her dread ineffable beauty,
Saw through texture fine of her clinging tunic
Blush the fire of flesh, the rose of her body,
Radiant, blinding;

Saw through filmy meshes the melting lovely
Flow of line, the exquisite curves, whence piercing
Rapture reached with tangible touch to thrill me,
Almost to slay me;

Saw the gleaming foot, and the golden sandal
Held by straps of Lydian work thrice doubled
Over the instep's arch, and up the rounded
Dazzling ankle;

Saw the charms that shimmered from knee to shoulder,
Hint of hues, than milk or the snowdrift whiter;
Secret grace, the shrine of the soul of passion,
Glows that consumed me;

Saw the gathered mass of her xanthic tresses,
Mitra-bound, escape from the clasping fillet,
Float and shine as clouds in the sunset splendor,
Mists in the dawn-fire;

Saw the face immortal, and daring greatly,
Raised my eyes to hers of unfathomed azure,
Drank their world's desire, their limitless longing,
Swooned and was nothing.

Sappho (b. 620 B.C.)

FEMININITY AND WOMANHOOD

Self Congratulation

Ellen, you were thoughtless once
Of beauty or of grace,
Simple and homely in attire,
Careless of form and face;
Then whence this change? and wherefore now
So often smoothe your hair?
And wherefore deck your youthful form
With such unwearied care?

Tell us, and cease to tire our ears
With that familiar strain;
Why will you play those simple tunes
So often o'er again?
'Indeed, dear friends, I can but say
That childhood's thoughts are gone;
Each year its own new feelings brings,
And years move swiftly on:

'And for these little simple airs –
I love to play them o'er
So much – I dare not promise, now,

To play them never more.'
I answered – and it was enough;
They turned them to depart;
They could not read my secret thoughts,
Nor see my throbbing heart.

I've noticed many a youthful form,
Upon whose changeful face
The inmost workings of the soul
The gazer well might trace;
The speaking eye, the changing lip,
The ready blushing cheek,
The smiling, or beclouded brow,
Their different feelings speak.

But, thank God! you might gaze on mine
For hours, and never know
The secret changes of my soul
From joy to keenest woe.
Last night, as we sat round the fire
Conversing merrily,
We heard, without, approaching steps
Of one well known to me!

There was no trembling in my voice,
No blush upon my cheek,
No lustrous sparkle in my eyes,
Of hope, or joy, to speak;
But, oh! my spirit burned within,
My heart beat full and fast!
He came not nigh – he went away –
And then my joy was past.

And yet my comrades marked it not:
My voice was still the same;
They saw me smile, and o'er my face
No signs of sadness came.
They little knew my hidden thoughts;
And they will NEVER know
The aching anguish of my heart,
The bitter burning woe!

Anne Brontë (1820–1849)

LOOK INTO THOUGHT

Look into thought and say what dost thou see,
Dive, be not fearful, how dark the waves flow,
Sink through the surge, and bring pearls up to me,
Deeper, ay, deeper; the fairest lie low.

I have dived, I have sought them, but none have I found,
In the gloom that closed o'er me no form floated by,
As I sunk through the void depths so black and profound
How dim died the sun and how far hung the sky!

What had I given to hear the soft sweep
Of a breeze bearing life through that vast realm of death!
Thoughts were untroubled and dreams were asleep,
The spirit lay dreadless and hopeless beneath.

Charlotte Brontë (1820–1849)

HOW CLEAR SHE SHINES

How clear she shines! How quietly
I lie beneath her guardian light;
While heaven and earth are whispering me,
'Tomorrow, wake, but, dream to-night.'
Yes, Fancy, come, my Fairy love!
These throbbing temples softly kiss;
And bend my lonely couch above,
And bring me rest, and bring me bliss.
The world is going; dark world, adieu!
Grim world, conceal thee till the day;
The heart thou canst not all subdue,
Must still resist, if thou delay!
Thy love I will not, will not share;
Thy hatred only wakes a smile;
Thy griefs may wound – thy wrongs may tear,
But, oh, thy lies shall ne'er beguile!
While gazing on the stars that glow
Above me, in that stormless sea,
I long to hope that all the woe
Creation knows, is held in thee!

Emily Brontë (1818–48)

A Lady Dressed by Youth

Her hair was curls of Pleasure and Delight,
Which on her brow did cast a glistening light.
As lace her bashful eyelids downward hung:
A modest countenance o'er her face was flung:
Blushes, as coral beads, she strung to wear
About her neck, and pendants for each ear:
Her gown was by Proportion cut and made,
With veins embroidered, with complexion laid,
Rich jewels of pure honor she did wear,
By noble actions brightened everywhere:
Thus dressed, to Fame's great court straightways she went,
To dance a brawl with Youth, Love, Mirth, Content.

Duchess of Newcastle Margaret Cavendish (1623–73)

A Letter of Thanks for the Precious Pearls

It is long – long – since my two eyebrows were painted like cassia-leaves. I have ended the adorning of myself. My tears soak my dress of coarse red silk. All day I sit in the Palace of the High Gate. I do not wash; I do not comb my hair. How can precious pearls soothe so desolate a grief.

Pan Chieh-Yü (c. A.D. 400)

A Letter to Rev. Convers Francis

Winslow [Maine], March 12, 1820

I can't talk about books, nor anything else, until I tell
you the good news; that I leave Norridgewock, and take a
school in Gardiner, as soon as the travelling is tolerable.
When I go to Gardiner, remember to write often, for 'it is
woman alone who truly feels what it is to be a stranger.' Did
you know that last month I entered my nineteenth year?

I hope, my dear brother, that you feel as happy as I do.
Not that I have formed any high-flown expectations. All
I expect is, that, if I am industrious and prudent I shall be
independent. I love to feel like Malcolm Graeme when he
says to Allan Bane, 'Tell Roderick Dhu I owe him naught.'

Have you seen 'Ivanhoe'? The 'Shakespeare of novelists' has
struck out a new path for his versatile and daring genius, I
understand. Does he walk with such elastic and lofty tread
as when upon his own mountain heath? Have his wings
expanded since he left the hills of Cheviot? Or was the
torch of fancy, lighted with the electric spark of genius,

extinguished in the waters of the Tweed? I have never seen it. Indeed 'I have na ony speerings' about the literary world, except through the medium of the newspapers. I am sorry to see the favored son of genius handled with such unmerciful, though perhaps deserved, severity in the review of 'Don Juan.' 'Lalla Rookh' is the last I have seen from the pen of 'Imagination's Charter'd Libertine.' I hope we shall have another collection of gems as splendid, and more pure, than his former collections.

Lydia Maria Child (1802–80)

A Letter to Miss Sarah Shaw

Upon receiving a donation to the anti-slavery cause, 1833

To Miss Sarah Shaw,

Your very unexpected donation was most gratefully received, though I was at first reluctant to take it, lest our amiable young friend had directly or indirectly begged the favor.

I am so great an advocate of individual freedom that I would have everything done voluntarily, nothing by persuasion. But Miss S assures me that you gave of your own accord, and this, though very unexpected, surprised me less than it would if I had not so frequently heard your brother speak of the kindness of your disposition.

We have good encouragement of success in the humble and unostentatious undertaking to which you have contributed. The zeal of a few seems likely to counterbalance the apathy of the many.

Posterity will marvel at the hardness of our prejudice on this subject, as we marvel at the learned and

conscientious believers in the Salem witchcraft. So
easy is it to see the errors of past ages, so difficult to
acknowledge our own!

With the kindest wishes for your happiness and
prosperity.

Lydia Maria Child (1802–80)

The Other Side of a Mirror

I sat before my glass one day,
And conjured up a vision bare,
Unlike the aspects glad and gay,
That erst were found reflected there –
The vision of a woman, wild
With more than womanly despair.
Her hair stood back on either side
A face bereft of loveliness.
It had no envy now to hide
What once no man on earth could guess.
It formed the thorny aureole
Of hard, unsanctified distress.

Her lips were open – not a sound
Came though the parted lines of red,
Whate'er it was, the hideous wound
In silence and secret bled.
No sigh relieved her speechless woe,
She had no voice to speak her dread.

And in her lurid eyes there shone
The dying flame of life's desire,
Made mad because its hope was gone,
And kindled at the leaping fire
Of jealousy and fierce revenge,
And strength that could not change nor tire.

Shade of a shadow in the glass,
O set the crystal surface free!
Pass – as the fairer visions pass –
Nor ever more return, to be
The ghost of a distracted hour,
That heard me whisper: – 'I am she!'

Mary Coleridge (1861-1907)

OUR LADY

Mother of God! no lady thou:
Common woman of common earth
Our Lady ladies call thee now,
But Christ was never of gentle birth;
A common man of the common earth.

For God's ways are not as our ways:
The noblest lady in the land
Would have given up half her days,
Would have cut off her right hand,
To bear the child that was God of the land.

Never a lady did He choose,
Only a maid of low degree,
So humble she might not refuse
The carpenter of Galilee:
A daughter of the people, she.

Out she sang the song of her heart.
Never a lady so had sung.
She knew no letters, had no art;
To all mankind, in woman's tongue,
Hath Israelitish Mary sung.

And still for men to come she sings,
Nor shall her singing pass away.
'He hath fillàd the hungry with good things' –
O listen, lords and ladies gay! –
'And the rich He hath sent empty away.'

Mary Coleridge (1861–1907)

EMANCIPATION

No rack can torture me,
My soul's at liberty
Behind this mortal bone
There knits a bolder one

You cannot prick with saw,
Nor rend with scymitar.
Two bodies therefore be;
Bind one, and one will flee.

The eagle of his nest
No easier divest
And gain the sky,
Than mayest thou,

Except thyself may be
Thine enemy;
Captivity is consciousness,
So's liberty.

Emily Dickinson (1830–86)

Renewal of Strength

And over the shadows of my life
Stole the light of a peace divine.
Oh! then my task was a sacred thing,
How precious it grew in my eyes!
'Twas mine to gather the bruised grain
For the 'Lord of Paradise.'

And when the reapers shall lay their grain
On the floors of golden light,
I feel that mine with its broken sheaves
Shall be precious in His sight.

Though thorns may often pierce my feet,
And the shadows still abide,
The mists will vanish before His smile,
There will be light at eventide.
The prison-house in which I live
Is falling to decay,
But God renews my spirit's strength,
Within these walls of clay.

Frances Harper (1825–1911)

The Volunteer's Thanksgiving

The last days of November, and everything so green!
A finer bit of country my eyes have never seen.
'Twill be a thing to tell of, ten years or twenty hence,
How I came down to Georgia at Uncle Sam's expense.

Four years ago this winter, up at the district school,
I wrote all day, and ciphered, perched on a white-pine stool;
And studied in my atlas the boundaries of the States,
And learnt the wars with England, the history and the dates.

Then little I expected to travel in such haste
Along the lines my fingers and fancy often traced,
To bear a soldier's knapsack, and face the cannon's mouth,
And help to save for Freedom the lovely, perjured South.

That red, old-fashioned school-house! what winds came
        sweeping through
Its doors from bald Monadnock, and from the mountains blue
That slope off south and eastward beyond the Merrimack!
O pleasant Northern river, your music calls me back
To where the pines are humming the slow notes of their psalm

Around a shady farm-house, half hid within their calm,
Reflecting in the river a picture not so bright
As these verandahed mansions, – but yet my heart's delight.

They're sitting at the table this clear Thanksgiving noon;
I smell the crispy turkey, the pies will come in soon, –
The golden squares of pumpkin, the flaky rounds of mince,
Behind the barberry syrups, the cranberry and the quince.

Be sure my mouth does water, – but then I am content
To stay and do the errand on which I have been sent.
A soldier mustn't grumble at salt beef and hard-tack:
We'll have a grand Thanksgiving if ever we get back!

I'm very sure they'll miss me at dinner-time today,
For I was good at stowing their provender away.
When mother clears the table, and wipes the platters bright,
She'll say, 'I hope my baby don't lose his appetite!'

But oh! the after-dinner! I miss that most of all, –
The shooting at the targets, the jolly game of ball,
And then the long wood-ramble! We climbed, and slid,
     and ran, –

We and the neighbor-children, – and one was Mary Ann,

Who (as I didn't mention) sat next to me at school:
Sometimes I had to show her the way to work the rule
Of Ratio and Proportion, and do upon her slate
Those long, hard sums that puzzle a merry maiden's pate.

I wonder if they're going across the hills today;
And up the cliffs I wonder what boy will lead the way;
And if they'll gather fern-leaves and checkerberries red,
And who will put a garland of ground-pine on her head.

O dear! the air grows sultry: I'd wish myself at home
Were it a whit less noble, the cause for which I've come.
Four years ago a school-boy; as foolish now as then!
But greatly they don't differ, I fancy, – boys and men.

I'm just nineteen to-morrow, and I shall surely stay
For Freedom's final battle, be it until I'm gray,
Unless a Southern bullet should take me off my feet. –
There's nothing left to live for, if Rebeldom should beat;

For home and love and honor and freedom are at stake,
And life may well be given for our dear Union's sake;

So reads the Proclamation, and so the sermon ran;
Do ministers and people feel it as soldiers can?

When will it all be ended? 'Tis not in youth to hold
In quietness and patience, like people grave and old:
A year? three? four? or seven? – O then, when I return,
Put on a big log, mother, and let it blaze and burn,

And roast your fattest turkey, bake all the pies you can,
And, if she isn't married, invite in Mary Ann!
Hang flags from every window! we'll all be glad and gay,
For Peace will light the country on that Thanksgiving Day.

Lucy Larcom (1824–93)

To Mrs. Celia Thaxter

Beverly, July 16, 1867

My dear Friend, – To think that yesterday I was among
the Enchanted Isles, and today here, with only the warm
murmur of the west wind among the elms! The glory of the
day and the far eastern sea lingers with me yet. How I do
thank you for those three bright days! The undercurrent of
memory would have been too much but for your kindness.

I think I kept it well covered, but there was a vast
unrest in me, all those days. I seemed to myself wandering
over the turfy slopes, and the rocks, and the sea, in search
of a dream, a sweet, impalpable presence that ever eluded
me. I never knew how fully dear Lizzie filled my heart, until
she was gone. Is it always so? But that Island is Lizzie to me,
now. It was the refuge of her dreams, when she could not
be there in reality. Her whole being seemed to blossom out
into the immense spaces of the sea. I am glad that I have
been there once again, and with only the dear brother,
and you whom she loved and admired so much. For you
are an enchantress. It is a great gift to attract and to *hold*
as you can, and rare, even among women. To some it is a
snare, but I do not believe it ever can be to you, because

the large generosity of the sea was born into you. How can
you help it, if your waves overblow with music, and all sorts
of mysterious wealth upon others of us humans? I hope you
beguiled our friend into a stay of more than the one day
he spoke of. It was doing him so much good to be there, in
that free and easy way; just the life he ought to lead for half
the year, at least. I shall always use my meagre arts most
earnestly to get him to the Island when you are there. There
is such a difference in human atmospheres, you know; the
petty, east-wind blighted inhabitants of towns are not good
for the health of such as he. I esteem it one of the wonderful
blessings of my life that he does not feel uncomfortable
when I am about. With you, there is the added element of
exhilaration, the rarest thing to receive, as one gets into
years. It is a sacred trust, the friendship of such a man.

Lucy Larcom (1824–93)

HAPPINESS

Happiness, to some, elation;
Is, to others, mere stagnation.
Days of passive somnolence,
At its wildest, indolence.
Hours of empty quietness,
No delight, and no distress.

Happiness to me is wine,
Effervescent, superfine.
Full of tang and fiery pleasure,
Far too hot to leave me leisure
For a single thought beyond it.
Drunk! Forgetful! This the bond: it
Means to give one's soul to gain
Life's quintessence. Even pain
Pricks to livelier living, then
Wakes the nerves to laugh again,
Rapture's self is three parts sorrow.
Although we must die to-morrow,
Losing every thought but this;
Torn, triumphant, drowned in bliss.

Happiness: We rarely feel it.
I would buy it, beg it, steal it,
Pay in coins of dripping blood
For this one transcendent good.

Amy Lowell (1874–1925)

Nurse Edith Cavell

Two o'clock, the morning of October 12th, 1915.
To her accustomed eyes
The midnight-morning brought not such a dread
As thrills the chance-awakened head that lies
In trivial sleep on the habitual bed.
'Twas yet some hours ere light;
And many, many, many a break of day
Had she outwatched the dying; but this night
Shortened her vigil was, briefer the way.
By dial of the clock
'Twas day in the dark above her lonely head.
'This day thou shalt be with Me.' Ere the cock
Announced that day she met the Immortal Dead.

Alice Meynell (1847–1922)

To O—, Of Her Dark Eyes

Across what calm of tropic seas,
'Neath alien clusters of the nights,
Looked, in the past, such eyes as these?
Long-quenched, relumed, ancestral lights!
The generations fostered them;
And steadfast Nature, secretwise –
Thou seedling child of that old stem –
Kindled anew thy dark-bright eyes.
Was it a century or two
This lovely darkness rose and set,
Occluded by grey eyes and blue,
And Nature feigning to forget?
Some grandam gave a hint of it –
So cherished was it in thy race,
So fine a treasure to transmit
In its perfection to thy face.
Some father to some mother's breast
Entrusted it, unknowing. Time
Implied, or made it manifest,
Bequest of a forgotten clime.
Hereditary eyes! But this

Is single, singular, apart: –
New-made thy love, new-made thy kiss,
New-made thy errand to my heart.

Alice Meynell (1847–1922)

EPITAPH

On her Son H.P. at St Syth's Church where her body also
   lies interred
What on Earth deserves our trust?
Youth and beauty both are dust
Long we gathering are with pain,
What one moment calls again.
Seven years childless marriage past,
A Son, a son is born at last:
So exactly lim'd and fair,
Full of good Spirits, Meen and Air,
As a long life is promised,
Yet, in less than six weeks dead.
Too promising, too great a mind
In so small room to be confined:
Therefore, as fit in heaven to dwell,
He quickly broke the Prison shell.
So subtle Alchemist,
Can't with Hermes Seal resist
The powerful spirit's subtler flight,
But t'will bid him long good night.
And so the Sun if it arise

Half so glorious as his Eyes,
Like this Infant, takes a shrowd
Buried in a morning Cloud.

Katherine Philips (1632–64)

On the Birthday of Queen Katherine

While yet it was the Empire of the Night,
And Stars still check'r'd Darkness with their Light,
From Temples round the cheerful Bells did ring,
But with the Peales a churlish Storm did sing.
I slumbr'd; and the Heavens like things did show,
Like things which I had seen and heard below.
Playing on Harps Angels did singing fly,
But through a cloudy and a troubl'd Sky,
Some fixt a Throne, and Royal Robes display'd,
And then a Massie Cross upon it laid.
I wept: and earnestly implor'd to know,
Why Royal Ensigns were disposed so.
An Angel said, The Emblem thou hast seen,
Denotes the Birthday of a Saint and Queen.

Ah, Glorious Minister, I then reply'd,
Goodness and Bliss together do reside
In Heaven and thee, why then on Earth below
These two combin'd so rarely do we know?
He said, Heaven so decrees: and such a Sable Morne
Was that, in which the *Son of God* was borne.

Then Mortal wipe thine Eyes, and cease to rave,
God darkn'd Heaven, when He the World did save.

Katherine Philips (1632–64)

The Mother's Hour

My little son would fain
Go from his mother never;

Leaves me with tender pain,
As parting were for ever.

I who have business,
The little cares of living,

Though small hands cling and press,
I send him from me grieving.

The little Love denied,
In passionate protestation

'Gainst her who shuts outside
His tender adoration.

Swift sands of gold that run
In Time's glass heaping, heaping,

Taking my little son
Out of his mother's keeping.

Time, there may come a time
He will not so approve me.

This is my golden clime,
In which the children love me.

Time, there may come a day,
Past prayers and interceding,

When he may turn away,
Deaf to my piteous pleading.

Katherine Philips (1632–64)

The Affinity

I have to thank God I'm a woman,
For in these ordered days a woman only
Is free to be very hungry, very lonely.

It is sad for Feminism, but still clear
That man, more often than woman, is pioneer.
If I would confide a new thought,
First to a man must it be brought.

Now, for our sins, it is my bitter fate
That such a man wills soon to be my mate,
And so of friendship is quick end:
When I have gained a love I lose a friend.

It is well within the order of things
That man should listen when his mate sings;
But the true male never yet walked
Who liked to listen when his mate talked.

I would be married to a full man,
As would all women since the world began;

But from a wealth of living I have proved
I must be silent, if I would be loved.

Now of my silence I have much wealth,
I have to do my thinking all by stealth.
My thoughts may never see the day;
My mind is like a catacomb where early Christians pray.

And of my silence I have much pain,
But of these pangs I have great gain;
For I must take to drugs or drink,
Or I must write the things I think.

If my sex would let me speak,
I would be very lazy and most weak;
I should speak only, and the things I spoke
Would fill the air awhile, and clear like smoke.

The things I think now I write down,
And some day I will show them to the Town.
When I am sad I make thought clear;
I can re-read it all next year.

I have to thank God I'm a woman,
For in these ordered days a woman only
Is free to be very hungry, very lonely.

Anna Wickham (1883–1947)

INDEX